BUT

If you are a school or amateur group, buy as many copies as you can afford, photocopy as many more as you need and have fun! There are no further fees.

I can be reached at ghjmep@live.co.uk if you would like to discuss any aspect of this play, or show interest in using it.

Cinderella and the Raiders of the Lost Slipper!

This is the first in a series of pantomime style plays called,

"New Comedies for all Stages"

There will, in the first series, be 7 {including the 3 published here}.
Each one will be longer than the last culminating in 3, 80-minute large cast pieces.

They were all written for use with the thousands of children I taught when I was head of a very successful drama department in the South East of England. A post I held for 16 years.

I hope you enjoy reading them and that many young people will enjoy being a part of future productions, as so many have in the past!

In this first volume you have two versions of Cinderella. A 5-minute homage to the Reduced Shakespeare Company and a longer piece in which you meet "The Raiders of the Lost Slipper" which actually fits one of the Ugly Sisters.

The third piece, grouped here because it's is also based on a traditional story, is my development of the story of "Goldilocks", which finally deals with the important questions, which are;
Why this young girl was wandering in the forest?
Why did she think it was OK to go into that strange house?

What happened after the Bears chased her away?
This version also brings in a New Pantomime Villain, the Nasty Nanny, "Gontaseed".

Come inside and join the fun!

Cinderella!

The 5-minute version

Ideal for assemblies or sketch show evenings.

Synopsis

A group of travelling players are due to perform their version of Cinderella at the Palace but the ugly sisters have been chosen to play rugby for England. Luckily two random ladies turn up and want to audition. Two audition scenes later; performed at breakneck speed {an homage to The Reduced Shakespeare Company} the Director accepts that they will simply have to do!

Cast list

The Director
Prince Charming
Buttons
Lady 1 {a man}
Lady 2 {another man}
Friend 1
Friend 2
Cinderella
Fairy Godmother
Voice {offstage}

A village square in front of the castle. A group of travelling players enter. The Director looks very depressed

Director: I am very depressed.

P. Charming: What's up? I thought we were ready to go.

Anyone: We were, but haven't you heard?

P. Charming: Heard what?

Anyone: About the Ugly Sisters!

P. Charming: What about the Ugly Sisters?

Anyone: They got picked to play for England, they're both playing prop forward at Twickenham tomorrow.

Director: Which leaves us high and dry, and we were meant to open at the Baron's Christmas Ball tomorrow... and he's not going to like it.

Buttons: He's not going to like it at all.

All: No! He's not going to like it at all!

Director: Oh, where am I going to find to two people ugly enough to play the Ugly Sisters at this short notice?

Enter two ladies {who should be played by men}

Lady 1: Ah, this looks like the place... and he is obviously in charge... Excuse me... Excuse me... Oih!

Buttons: Yes?

Lady 1: We are beautiful ladies. {*To audience: "oh yes we are!" and so on*}. In search of suitable employment.

Lady 2: We have come in response to your advertisement.

Buttons: What? But you can't have, I only placed it yesterday and it didn't mention "Ladies". Show me.

They do

Oh, you don't want me, you want him.

Lady 1:   Oh, you mean he's the Director?

Buttons: I know, hard to believe isn't it.

Lady 2:   Never mind, he'll have to do.

They go over

Lady 1:   Good morning.

Director: Huh... good morning. What Can I do for you?

Lady 2:   We are beautiful ladies, and we have come to audition for your play.

Lady 1:   We wish to be stars. We wish to tread the silver road to fame and fortune. We want to be on "Britain's Got Talent", and we're told you can help, and these two want to be in the chorus, don't you.

Other two: Oh yes, we do, certainly, yes!

Director:	I can help, I know I can, but you'll have to audition first. What can you do?
Lady 1:	I can sing.
No. 1:	So can I.
Lady 2:	I can dance a little.
No. 2:	So can I.
Director:	But can you act?
Ladies:	Um... well.... Not very well.
Other two:	No, not at all, never have been able too. Always wanted too, but... no.
Director:	Marvellous, you'll fit in perfectly.
Rest of cast:	Oih!!!!
Director:	Only joking.
Rest of cast:	Humph, that's all right then.

Director: Right, it's comedy we're interested in, so tell us your best joke, and if we laugh, you're in.

They tell jokes. If the audience don't laugh the Director falls about instead

Director: Excellent, wonderful, stupendous, you're in. Let's rehearse. OK cast. Act 1 SC 5, "The Kitchen Scene", followed immediately by Act 3 Sc 5, "Does the slipper fit?" Positions everybody! Now this *{pointing at nothing}* is a large fireplace, we're in the kitchen, it's stone, it's dank, it's cold and it's early in the morning. Cinders is scrubbing the floor, and Buttons is polishing his brass. OK, and lights, AND LIGHTS, oh whatever, and ACTION!

Cinders: Oh Buttons, I do so hate scrubbing the floor with an old toothbrush.

Buttons: I know it's hard Cinders, but don't be sad, I'm here.

Cinders: I know.

Buttons: Oh! Have you heard about the Ball?

Cinders: The Ball at the Palace?

Buttons: Yes!

Cinders: No.

Buttons: There's going to be a Ball at the Palace, everybody is going to be there.

You could insert some celebrity names here. Ending with one of your group

Cinders: Everyone except us.

Buttons: But Cinders, I wouldn't expect to go, I'm only the Bellboy, and if I can't go, surely, you wouldn't want to.

Cinders: *{Obviously not meaning it}* No, of course not.

Enter the two ladies, as the Ugly Sisters and the other two

Lady 1:   Cinderella!

Lady 2:   Cinderella!

Together: CINDERELLA!

Director: No, no, no, no... no. That's no good
               at all. *{To Lady 1}* You're just not ugly
               enough.

Lady 2:   What about me?

Director: You're fine.

Lady 2:   Well really, I've never been so
               insulted!

Director: No? You should get out more... Now
               you, you've got to understand what
               motivates your character... You're twisted
               with envy!

*Throughout this sequence the lady over acts all the
               things mentioned*

Lady 1:   Envy!

Director: You're driven by Greed!

Lady 1:   Greed!

Director: You want to marry the Prince, but you know you never will!

Lady 1:   Oh, that's so sad.

Director: That's it, hold that feeling... Now, again!

Lady 2:   Cinderella!

Lady 1:   *{Like Quasimodo}* Cindereelllaaa.

Director: Brilliant!... Sorry, carry on.

Cinders: Yes?

Lady 1:   Shall we tell her?

Lady 2:   *{Smugly}* I think we should.

Lady 1:   We've been invited to the Ball.

Lady 2:   Yes. To meet the Prince.

Lady 1:	But you aren't coming.
Lady 2:	No, you aren't coming.
Other two:	Even we're going and you're not.
Cinders:	Do I look bothered, I mean, do I look bothered?
All:	Yes
Lady 1:	So, get out my best blue frock.
Lady 2:	And my best ruby necklace.
Lady 1:	And my best diamond tiara.
Both:	And then get on with that floor.

They move away and pretend to talk

Cinders:	Oh Buttons!
Buttons:	Oh Cinders!
Director:	Oh well, it'll have to do. Act 3 Scene

5, "Does the slipper fit". Positions and...
Action!

P. Charming: I have invited all the ladies in the land to my palace, to see if I can find my Princess, for I know only one foot would be fair enough to fit this beautiful slipper *{use a comical item like a welly}* Bring on all the ladies in the land.

Offstage: Bring on all the ladies in the land. Etc.

The members of the cast, including Buttons all try the shoe on. It fits Buttons and he is bustled off. Eventually Cinders puts it on

P. Charming: Oh, my Princess!

Cinders: Oh, my Prince!

They go to embrace but she treads on his toe

P. Charming: Oh, my foot!

Director: OK hold it there... You'll do. You're all in. Now, we've only got 24 hours before we perform, so we're going to go for a quick run through. Top speed, no breaks, and plenty of audience reaction please. You lot, play all the other parts.

This should be done as fast as you can manage it with props flying about and live costume changes

Cinders: Oh, I'm so sad, my evil stepmother and two ugly sisters are making my life a misery.

Enter ladies

Both: Cinders!

Lady 1: Clean the sink!

Lady 2: Make the beds!

Lady 1: Polish the shoes!

Both: And don't forget the lavatory!

Buttons: Poor Cinders, I love her so!

Voice: Ball, Ball, invitations for all!

Ladies: Yes please!

Buttons: I'll get one for Cinders!

Ladies: We're going to the Ball and you're not!

Cinders: Boo Hoo!

Buttons: Don't worry Cinders dear, here's your ticket.

Cinders: Oh Buttons, but I can't go looking like this.

Fairy Godmother: Never fear, here is your frock and the coach is outside.

Cinders: Oh, thank you!

Fairy Godmother: But be back by midnight!

At the Ball.

P. Charming: Oh, my beautiful Princess!

Cinders: Oh, my handsome Prince!

The clock strikes midnight

Cinders: EEK! I must flee!

P. Charming: No, don't go! Oh Rats.. Oh look... a glass slipper *{A Wellington boot, he sniffs it and grimaces}* This is my way to happiness! Call all the ladies in the land!

All: Call all the ladies in the land!

The slipper routine again but really fast, followed by a big embrace and freeze.

Director: And they all lived happily ever after, except Buttons... Ahhh!

All: Ahh.

THE END

Cinderella And the Raiders Of The Lost Slipper.

{A pint-sized panto}

Synopsis
This pantlet {yes, this is a made up word!} opens in the traditional way with the usual range of characters, until that is the slipper fits the wrong foot and, in any case, is found to belong to the Raiders of the Lost Slipper who have come to claim back what is rightly theirs!
Ideal for learning the tricks of the panto trade or as the climax of an evening of comedy!

Cast List

Cinderella
Buttons
The two ugly sisters
The Nasty Stepmother
Baron Hard-up
Buttons Assistant
Fairy Godmother
Prince
Raiders
Improvisations involving characters of your choice during the journey to the Palace

Scene 1
The Kitchen

Cinderella: Oh boo hoo, boo hoo, boo.......hoo. I am so, so sad in so many different ways. Ever since Daddy, Baron Hard-up, married my new "Stepmother" and she moved in with her two ugly, pongy, self-obsessed, super-lazy daughters my life has been a misery. I can't get near the Playstation 4, I can't get near the x box, and as for the 4K TV, forget it. I'm missing "I'm a celebrity" EVERY night. They've cancelled my dance lessons, they've cancelled my riding classes, they've stopped me learning Mandarin Chinese and now I spend all my days just cleaning, cleaning, cleaning with this *{holds up a toothbrush}* and my only friends are the mice, and I'm frightened of mice....

Buttons: I'll be your friend Cinderella, I will, honest I will!

Cinderella: I know you would Buttons, but you are only a bus boy and don't have so much as an ISA to protect us against an uncertain future in these times of unstable pension funds and increasing austerity.

Buttons: I know dear Cinderella, but I do have a cockney accent, natural charm and a cheeky grin... I know, we'll try and cheer you up, won't we boys and girls!

There follows an improvisation with the audience based around passing a parcel. Cinderella wins, the prize is a rat

Cinderella: Oh, thank you. *{Buttons tries to look sweet. Enter the Evil Stepmum and the Ugly Sisters. These can be boys. They kick Buttons off the stage. He exits looking miserable and playing the crowd for sympathy}.*

Stepmum: Cinderella!

Ugly Sisters: Cinderella! Where are you! It's time to clean the shoes, and the stove, and the floor and the TOILETS, and to make the beds and the lunch and the dinner and to cut the lawns with THESE *{they hold up a pair of nail scissors}.*

Cinderella: Oh, why are you so mean to me? Is it because you were neglected as babies?

Between each reason the Sisters adopt a different comic thoughtful pose then speak

Cinderella: Is it because nature has not graced you with the good looks even of a Pomeranian pug?

Sisters: Ahhh, No!

Cinderella: Is it because no perfume in the world can mask the faint odour of SPROUTS?

Sisters: No, it is none of those. We're just NOT VERY NICE, are we boys and girls!... See, even they've worked it out and they've only known us 2 minutes, dimwit, now get on with your chores.

Cinderella gets down on her knees and begins to scrub the stage with a toothbrush. Buttons re-enters with a letter

Buttons: A letter, a letter, and it's from the Palace!

The Stepmum and Sisters take it in turn to hold it. It is obviously upside down etc. They cannot read

Stepmum: Oh, you read it Buttons! I haven't got my glasses!

Sisters: And neither have we!

Buttons takes out a ridiculous pair of glasses and puts them carefully on, he holds the letter at various distances but eventually gives in

Buttons: It's no good, it's written in Posh. I don't read Posh.

Cinderella: Oh for goodness sake, give it to me *{She takes out an even more ridiculous pair of glasses and begins to read in an extremely posh English voice}* "Their Majesties, The King and Queen, would like to invite Baron Hard-up and his entire family to a Ball at the Palace this very night in order to select a suitable bride for Crown Prince Barry. The wedding is scheduled for a week Tuesday. Kick-off is at 8."
Oh, how exciting! A Ball, and a Wedding! What shall I wear?

Stepmum and Sisters: You don't need to worry about that young lady because YOU are not going! The very thought of it!

Baron Hard-up enters. He is very nice but not very strong willed

Cinderella: Oh Daddy, there is to be a Ball at the Palace and THEY *{pointing an accusing finger}* WON'T LET ME GO, WHICH IS VERY MEAN, isn't it, boys and girls.

There follows an improvised "oh yes it is, oh no it isn't sequence which the Stepmum ends with

Stepmum: Oh, do be quiet! No one cares what you think anyway, you are only "the audience" and we are... proper characters! *{The audience boos}.*

The Stepmum and Sisters leave babbling on about what they are going to wear. Buttons stands to the side of the stage and the Baron puts his arm around Cinderella

Baron Hard-up: Not to worry Cinders dear, when my new "wife" and her "delightful" daughters are gone we can have a nice game of Scrabble.

Cinderella: Oh Daddy! You just don't understand!

Cinders rushes off followed by the Baron saying

Baron: It could be Cluedo if you prefer, I'm sure I have that somewhere.

Buttons: Poor old Cinders, nothing nice ever happens to her. I know! I'll help her out by making a nice lunch. I'm good at cooking I am. *{Line could change to "*I know, I'll give her room a super makeover, I'm good at interior design I am" *if you go with option 2}.*

Buttons exits with enthusiasm

Optional Insert
This is a completely improvised piece involving Buttons and his Assistant trying to cook a meal. Traditionally it would involve odd ingredients, silly errors, and things almost thrown into the audience, custard pie jokes and flour.
The alternative could be a slapstick decorating sequence as they give her room a modern makeover, badly

Meanwhile back in the main plot

Scene 2
This can be front of curtain

Cinderella: Oh, me oh my, and I did so want to go to the Ball!

Fairy Godmother: *{Appearing in a flash}* And you shall go to the Ball for I am your Fairy Godmother and I am MAGIC!

Cinderella: Oh, thank you Fairy Godmother, again, I just hope you are a bit more successful than last time.

Fairy Godmother: Live and learn dear, live and learn. Now get these on and the carriage is waiting outside!

The scene now changes. Cinderella is on her way to the Palace. During her journey she can meet any number of characters. Del Boy selling some beans to Jack, Dick Whittington lost, or anything you like really. This is the joy of Panto. One group should be a group of Baddies who are the Raiders of the Lost Slipper

Scene 3
At the Palace. People are dancing; the Ugly Sisters are trying to get the attention of Crown Prince Barry

Sisters: Oh Princikins, can we please have the next dance! Pretty please!

Prince: *{Aside}* There's nothing pretty about those two!... Later dear Ladies, later... *{Aside}* A lot later if I have anything to do with it!

Enter Cinderella with Buttons, Baron Hard-up and the Fairy Godmother

Prince: Wowsa, wowsa, now that's what I call a beauty!

Fairy Godmother: Oh, thank you Barry, it's been so long since anyone called me beautiful!

Prince: Not you! Her! Haven't you read the script!

Fairy Godmother: Sorry, silly me.

The Prince approaches Cinderella and they dance. Everyone reacts in character. After a little while a clock strikes. The Fairy Godmother rushes over to Cinders and whispers, loudly, in her ear

Fairy Godmother: Oh dear, I'm so sorry, forgot to mention, the rental, hum, magic, runs out at Midnight. You must leave!

Cinderella: Oh, Fairy Godmother! *{She runs out leaving a glass slipper. Crown Prince Barry picks it up}.*

Prince: I will marry no other than the Princess whose foot fits this elegant slipper {*probably an old boot*}

Leave me all of you, I will visit every home in the land tomorrow to find my one true love and seal my destiny with Loves true kiss! {*The Sisters swoon as the lights go out*}.

Scene 4

The following morning in the drawing room of Baron Hard-ups home.

Baron: Oh, I do hope the Prince finds that the slipper fits one of you! It would be so nice to be father-in-law to the Future King, such a nice young man.

Stepmum: And so rich!

Enter the Prince

Prince: Come forward all the ladies of the land and try on this beautiful slipper!

The sisters come forward, as does the Stepmum, much to the surprise of the Baron. When the Second Sister tries it on, it fits, she shrieks and is pushed over by the Prince who wrestles it off her foot

Prince: Are there no others! This is the last house! She must be here!

Buttons: *{Aside}* Even though I am secretly in love with Cinderella *{to audience}* Did you know that? Really? You did? Oh well. I must not be selfish! *{out loud}* Prince! There is another *{he steps forward causing some confusion}* Cinderella has been locked in the cellar because they are jealous of her great beauty!

Prince: Bring her forth now!

Cinderella emerges and they are about to place the slipper on her foot when the Raiders of the Lost Slipper burst in

Raiders: Hold it right there Princy. You know as well as we do that that slipper belongs to us!

Prince: But I've never seen you before in my life!

Raiders: Really? So you don't remember this?

The Prince is shown the contents of a small box

Prince: Gasp! You mean that was you?

Raiders: Yes! And now we have come to claim what is rightfully ours! Hand over the slipper or the Ugly Sisters get it! *{Custard Pies are held menacingly}*.

Prince: All right! you can have the slipper, but give it to them anyway. *{The custard pies are flung}*.

The Raiders grab the slipper and lots of other stuff and leave

Baron Hard-up: Well that was an unexpected twist to the plot and such as like and no mistake! Whatever shall we do now?

Sister: Well you did say you would marry the one that the slipper fitted...

Prince: Nooooooooooo... *{As the lights fade to black, the Princes cry of despair echoes around the theatre}*.

The End

Goldilocks and the Three Bears!
{The Panto}

Synopsis

As the Storyteller points out, the story of Goldilocks isn't really a story at all, just an episode. In this version Goldilocks runs off into the Forest to escape from her evil Nanny, Gontaseed, and mistakes the recently arrived Polar bears house for her friends' forest Den. The bears return from their morning walk and the traditional part of the tale unfolds. When Goldilocks runs off the bears give chase, in a friendly sort of way, and everyone ends up back in the village square where Gontaseed gets her just deserts, and who would want mushy peas for dessert!

Cast list

Storyteller
Gontaseed {the Dame}
Goldilocks
Poppy, her friend
Daddy Bear
Mummy Bear
Baby Bear
Child 1
Child 2
Child 3
Child 4
Smallest Child
Village children {no lines}

Prologue
This first sequence can be set front of curtain and nowhere in particular.

Storyteller: Hello Boys and Girls! I said, "Hello Boys and Girls" *{etc.}* that's better. I am The Storyteller and I am very, very old, as you can probably tell! Today I am going to tell you the story of Goldilocks and the Three Bears, with the help of some of my friends... The trouble is that the story of Goldilocks and the Three Bears isn't really a story at all, more of a chapter really or even just an episode... I mean, so many questions just aren't answered! Why was a little girl called Goldilocks wandering in the forest in the first place? What possessed her to break into the only house she saw? How was it that that house was the home to a family of Bears? What happened to Goldilocks when she fled into the trees and did the Three Bears just let it go {sorry.} Well I'm a proper storyteller as storytellers go and I like to tell proper stories with a beginning and a middle and an end so that's what I am going to do! Ladies and Gentlemen, boys and girls, the real and "true" story of "GOLDILOCKS AND THE THREE BEARS."

Scene 1

The curtains open to reveal a town square, a group of children are playing a tag sort of game and there is laughter and joy in the air {they could be dancing if you prefer!} Suddenly a loud and horrid voice fills the square!

Gontaseed: GOLDILOCKS! ARE YOU PLAYING WITH THOSE "ORDINARY" CHILDREN AGAIN? BECAUSE IF YOU ARE...

Goldilocks: Quick, run, there's no escape for me but if Gontaseed catches you you'll be scrubbing the square for a week! Oh, why does she have to be so horrible!

Poppy: Just come with us Goldilocks! We can hide you in the Forest in our special camp and that horrid old hag will never find you ever again.

Goldilocks: That is kind of you Poppy, but what about Daddy and little Mya, I could never leave them at the mercy of that Dragon!

Poppy: All right Goldilocks, but if you change your mind you know where to find us, in the clearing beyond The Old Oak. If you get to The Yew Tree, you'll know you've gone too far.

Gontaseed: *{As she enters}* Be gone, the lot of you! Before you make me even crosser than I already am.

The children flee. Gontaseed circles menacingly around Goldilocks

Gontaseed: So, Goldilocks, playing with the PEASANTS again. What would your Father have to say!

Goldilocks: Nothing since you took over as Nanny and made everything so scary. Why can't you just be nice for once! We were only playing a game in the sunshine and there's nothing wrong with that!

Gontaseed: Don't you dare answer me back young Lady! You don't know how lucky you are to get a Nanny of my Cal-eye-bar and training. The house was falling apart till I turned up! People having fun left, right and centre, sweets and chocolate everywhere! Outrageous!

Goldilocks: It's not outrageous is it boys and girls!

Gontaseed: Oh yes it is!

The usual sequence develops. When the time is right Gontaseed ends it by saying...

Gontaseed: Oh, be quiet! Nobody cares what you think because YOU, are children and should be seen, occasionally, and never heard!

Goldilocks leads the Boos

Gontaseed: Oh, I've had enough of this! I'm going back to the nursery to break some more toys! As for you Goldilocks, get yourself to the market and buy my dinner! You're having Mushy Peas, again, and you will every night until you eat them all with a smile on your face. Ha, Ha, ha!

Gontaseed exits

Goldilocks: Oh, what shall I do Boys and Girls? Shall I go to the market and get Gontaseed's dinner and go home and eat Mushy Peas, again, or shall I go into the forest and find the clearing past The Old Oak and meet up with Poppy and the others and live happily ever after? What's that you say? *Go And Eat The Mushy Peas*? I don't think so. It's the forest for me! Wish me luck boys and girls! The forest can be a dangerous place so I must be very careful!

Scene 2

Storyteller: {Front of curtain} So Goldilocks wandered off into the forest by herself, which was a very silly thing to do! She wandered about for ages until she passed an Old Oak, but was it "The" Old Oak? Only time would tell!

The curtains open to reveal the house of the three Polar bears. I see these in Polar Bear Onsies. They do need to be Polar bears unless you drop out some of the lines

Mummy Bear: Oh, Daddy Bear, you are so clever. Fancy finding this lovely cave in the middle of the forest after we walked all the way from Svalbard.

Baby Bear: {studiously reading} Mummy, this is not a cave, it's a house, and if I'm not mistaken it probably belongs to someone else... look at all these personal touches. {Holds up something funny. You decide based on your audience}.

Daddy Bear: Well let's not worry about that now. I'm sure we made the right decision to come and live here. Our ice was "floeing" away at an alarming rate.

Baby Bear: Daddy, really? "Floeing away."

Mummy Bear: Never you mind about Daddy Bear's jokes Baby Bear. Lunch is almost ready, and you need to wash your paws.

Baby Bear: Oh, all right Mummy Bear. *{Baby Bear exits briefly and re-enters after the exchange between Daddy and Mummy}.*

Mummy Bear: Oh, Daddy Bear, I do hope we made the right decision coming here.

Daddy Bear: I'm sure we did dear. There's plenty of fish in the streams and berries on the trees, and I'm sure the local Bears will accept us after a while.

Mummy Bear: I do hope so Daddy Bear. We do stand out so being Polar Bears.

Baby Bear: Is lunch ready Mummy Bear? What is it?

Mummy Bear: It's your favourite Baby Bear! Porridge!

Baby Bear and Daddy Bear: Porridge! Yummy!

They sit down to eat. Baby Bear takes a mouthful and jumps up making a real fuss about how hot it is. You can't overdo this. Eventually

Daddy Bear: I think it's a little hot dear.

Mummy Bear: Ah, yes. It's this new stove you see. It actually works.

Daddy Bear: I know, let's go for a walk in the Forest whilst the porridge cools down! It's always good to take exercise before breakfast and we might make some new friends!

The bears all put on their dark glasses because everywhere is hot to a Polar bear, except the North Pole, and exit. As they leave Goldilocks opens the door and puts her head around it

Goldilocks: Hello, hello. Is there anybody there? Oh, there's nobody in. Oh well I did pass The Old Oak and I haven't passed The Yew Tree so this must be the special camp that Poppy told me about *{Goldilocks begins to explore. She could find odd and amusing things and ask the audience what they think they are for [a car horn, a party popper, a pair of old socks] or just get straight to the porridge}* Oh look! Three bowls of Porridge! That's my favourite. I haven't had porridge since stinky old Gontaseed turned up. I'm going to try some! *{she does}* Yurgh, that's much too hot. Bleurgh, that's much too salty....Hmmm, this ones just right *{she gobbles the bowl with no manners at all}* Now I need to sit down, Oh, three chairs, let's try this chair... Ooh, that's far too high, it's making me giddy!... Argh, that caused a bruise!...let's try the little one *{she does and it disintegrates and she falls to the floor}* Oh dear, I've broken it! I'll have to get a new one as soon as I can!... *{yawning}* Ohhhh, I'm soo tired, I think I'll see if I can find somewhere to lie down. *{She goes to wherever the beds are}* Goodness, three beds, the springs are poking through on this one!......Woah, this one almost swallowed me... Ahhhh, just right, I think I'll take a little snooze whilst I'm waiting for Poppy and the others...

Goldilocks begins to snore comically, snuffles a bit and then is quiet. The Three Bears come back in and go to sit at the table

Mummy Bear: Come along then, let's enjoy our wholesome breakfast!

Daddy Bear: Mummy Bear? Shouldn't we enrich it with added Omega 3 fish oils and other appropriate nutrients?

Mummy Bear: Perhaps we should Daddy Bear *{she opens a cupboard or bag and takes out the largest plastic fish you can manage. As she is about to stick it in the porridge Daddy Bear says...}.*

Daddy Bear: Hold on Mummy Bear! Somebody has been eating my porridge!

Mummy Bear: Goodness Daddy Bear, you're right! And somebody has been eating my porridge!

Baby Bear: Yaaaahhhhhh. And somebody has been eating my porridge AND IT'S ALL GONE...

Daddy Bear: And somebody has been sitting in my chair!

Mummy Bear: Goodness, and somebody has been sitting in my chair!

Baby Bear: And somebody has been sitting in my chair AND IT'S ALL BROKEN UP! WAAAAH.

Daddy Bear: This is terrible! We must have been burgled! I knew we should have locked the door. It's not like the old country!... Perhaps somebody saw them!

Mummy Bear: Perhaps they did Daddy Bear *{referring to the audience}*.

Daddy Bear: Eek! Who are they?

Baby Bear: They, Daddy Bear, are the audience, and they are very nice, aren't you boys and girls? *{The audience responds}* Have you seen the naughty burglar who broke into our house? You have? Do you know where they are? In the cupboard, you say? *{Mummy and Daddy Bear check each location. You can adapt this depending on your set}* Under the chair? In the matchbox? *{They all look}* Yeurgh! Oh... you said in the bed! *{They stealthily creep up on Daddy Bears bed and leap on it. As they do Goldilocks springs out of Baby Bears bed and there is a comedy chase sequence, ideally with a strobe and silent movie chase music. Goldilocks eventually runs off into the wings doing a comedy fading scream effect}*.

Daddy Bear: Quick. Let's follow her!

Mummy Bear: Yes. I think we frightened her, and she was only a little girl!

Baby Bear: We don't want people to think that we are mean or nasty! We've only been here for two months and we'd hate to be sent back to the North Pole!

They exit quickly in the same direction as Goldilocks. Baby Bear comes back in to collect his favourite cute teddy and then re-exits

Scene 3

Storyteller: *{Front of Curtain}* So now everyone was over excited and worried! Gontaseed had realised that Goldilocks was missing when she called her for her lunch of Mushy Peas and nobody came. Poppy realised that Goldilocks was missing when she returned from the actual hiding place past the right Old Oak and found the square empty. Goldilocks realised that she had done a bad thing, even though she didn't mean to, and the Three Bears were worried that they had frightened a little girl when they thought she was a big bad burglar hiding in Baby Bears bed. As luck would have it, they were all heading for the same place. Right here!

Back in the village square. Poppy runs in with other children. They have been searching for Goldilocks. You can divide the children's lines amongst as many children as you need to

Poppy: Oh no, Goldilocks isn't here!

Child 1: Did you tell her the way to the camp PROPERLY Poppy.

Poppy: I think I did.

Child 2: You know you're always getting your left mixed up with your right.

Child 3: And you're Oak Tree mixed up with your Sycamore.

Poppy: No, I definitely did tell her right. Oh, I do hope she hasn't gotten lost or met anyone horrid. I should have waited and taken her myself!

Child 4: Well there's no point blaming yourself. We'll just have to spread out and find her before that horrible Gontaseed catches on.

Gontaseed enters at this point. When she speaks the children look theatrically scared

Gontaseed: Before that horrible Gontaseed catches on to what? You puny little peasant kids! It's easy to see that you don't eat your Mushy Peas!

Poppy and the children: Oh, but we do Miss Gontaseed, and our blueberries and our melon and our fruit juice 5 times a day.

Smallest child: And we are very careful to remain fully hydrated at all times to maximise our digestive and brain functions! *{big cheesy smile}*.

Gontaseed: Ah, but do you floss every time you eat!
Poppy: Ah... no.

Gontaseed: Ha! I thought as much. Now stop trying to distract me, what is it that you don't want horrid old me to catch on to!

Child 1: It's Goldilocks, she's... missing!

Gontaseed: I thought as much! Tell me everything you know, right now.

Smallest Child: Well, the largest lake in the world by volume is Lake Baikal. The laws of gravity were discovered by Isaac Newton and Columbus sailed the Ocean Blue in 1492.

Everyone looks at the child with a mixture of disbelief and expectation

Gontaseed: And?

Smallest Child: That's all I've got... Oh come on I'm only 7 *{or insert age}* gimme a break.

Gontaseed: Worrying, definitely worrying. Right, you're going to help me find Goldilocks before her peas go cold whether you like it or not and so are you {*the audience, the children prompt them in to an "Oh no were not" sequence which Gontaseed ends with:*} If you don't then you have to eat the Mushy Peas USING celery sticks! Now, Poppy you go in that...

At this point Goldilocks bursts in

Goldilocks: {*Shouting*} Bear, Bear! {*The children shrug and start to undress*} Not that sort of Bare, Polar Bears, 3 of them, they're after me and they aren't very far behind!

In a panic all the children try to hide behind Gontaseed stage right. Gontaseed pulls them around and hides behind them

Gontaseed: Try and look big and ferocious, Bears aren't very clever, and you might confuse them!

Goldilocks: But you are much bigger than us! Why can't we hide behind you!

Gontaseed: Because I have a qualification on Forest First Aid! And it looks like you might need it! Quick, they're coming!

The Three Bears come running in stage left. As they enter the children draw themselves up and wave their arms and bare their teeth and roar. The three bears skid to a halt and huddle together

Baby Bear: What's that! I don't think I've ever seen one of those before!

Mummy Bear: I don't know dear. Perhaps we'd better ask it. Daddy Bear?

Daddy Bear: Oh dear, oh all right then… I will *{he steps forward tentatively}* Ah, hello, ah, can you help us… We are looking for a girl with long golden hair.

Mummy Bear: Who was hiding in Baby bears bed and I'm afraid we frightened her.

Baby Bear: By mistake and she ran off and I think she thought we were chasing her because we were angry or something.

Daddy Bear: But we're not angry and we only eat porridge and the occasional fish and you don't look like a fish so… yes.

The children stop waving their arms and talk to each other

Poppy: Did you understand that? Just sounded like a load of old growling to me.

Goldilocks: Don't worry, I used my Google Translator App. They said they were looking for me to say sorry for frightening me.

Poppy: Then you can use it to tell them that you thought that their house was our camp and then we can all live happily ever after!

Daddy Bear: That's all right, we have that App too and understand everything you are saying!

Gontaseed: But what about me?

Goldilocks: What about you?

Gontaseed: I'm the pantomime villain! I can't be part of a Happy Ever After! It wouldn't be right.

Poppy: Hmmm, you're right.

Smallest Child: I know! *{they huddle and deliver the next dialogue as asides}* I can use my 12-megapixel phone camera to take Gontaseed's picture then I can photoshop it on to a picture of a really ugly fish and then show it to the Bears and they can EAT her!

Goldilocks: Oh dear, that is a bit harsh. I know she isn't a very nice Nanny, but I don't think she deserves to be eaten by a bear!

Smallest Child: Not even a little bit?

Goldilocks: No, definitely not.

Child 2: How about the Bears? They might have a good idea.

They all huddle together and have an animated discussion with lots of visual twisting of hair and Chinese burns and pushing off cliffs and stuff until Baby Bear says;

Baby Bear: Got it?

All: *{Except Gontaseed each time}* What?

Baby Bear whispers something to them. They all turn to the audience, grin together, rub their hands and say;

All: Hmmmm. Mushy Peas. Poetic!

Goldilocks: Gontaseed!

Gontaseed: Yes?

Goldilocks: You have been a very naughty Nanny!

Gontaseed: I know! And do you know what?

All: What?
Gontaseed: I did it on purpose!

All: Gasp!

Goldilocks: Come on audience, "Gasp!" *{they do}* and so there's only one thing for it! Bring on the Mushy Peas! *{This should be as big a bucket of lumpy green slime as you can manage. Gontaseed is sat on a chair. The audience are encouraged to get involved in the countdown and then pour it over her head to a chorus of "Yeurghs and Bleurghs".*

Storyteller: And so, our story ends! A proper story with good guys and bad guys and misunderstandings and beginnings and middles and stuff. We hope you have enjoyed it and remember; bears aren't always what they seem to be! Bye.

All: Bye, Bye *{waving as they retreat up the stage and the curtains close.}*

The End

Also by Gareth Jones

Non-Fiction
On This Day for Teachers
Saving the Planet, one step at a time {as "Plays in the Rain"}
Dealer's Choice, The Home Poker Game Handbook
Mametz Wood, Three Stories of Wales {First published by Bretwalda}
Outstanding School Trip Leadership
Top Teacher Tips for Outstanding Behaviour for Learning {as Gethin James}
Cheeky Elf Solutions for Busy Parents
A Short Report on the Planet known locally as Earth {as Abel Star}
Make Your Own Teepee
Travelling with Children {First published by Bretwalda. Now in its second edition and fully illustrated}
Identifying Gifted and Talented Children, and what to do next
Outstanding Transition, A Teacher's Guide
An Unofficial set of revision notes for the Edexcel GCSE, History B, American West
An Unofficial set of revision notes for the Edexcel GCSE, History B, Medicine Unit
The Big Activity Book for KS3 Drama {published by ZigZag}
The Drama Handbook KS2 {this is an age adapted version of the above. They should not be bought together}
Personal Learning Project Guide {March 2020}

Short Stories
The Christmas Owls {Based on an idea by Millie Carzana}
The Pheasant that Refused to Fly {includes "The Cave." Winner of the 2018 Hailsham Arts Festival Short Story Competition}

The Unicorns of Moons Hill and the Broken Heart {Based on an idea by Millie Carzana}

An Owl called Moonlight and The Midnight Tree {Based on an idea by Millie Carzana}

The Amazing Adventures of Edwina Elf {Based on an idea by Millie Carzana}

A Mermacorn Christmas Adventure {Based on an idea by Millie Carzana}

"A Shirt for Mr De Niro" and other Stories

Hailsham Festival Anthology 2019 {Edited by}

Plays

Georgina and the Dragon {First published by Schoolplay}

Jason and the Astronauts {Also first published by Schoolplay}

William Shakespeare's Romeo and Juliet, A new adaption for KS2 and KS3

Dr Milo's Experiment

GET SANTA! From the original East Sussex film project

The Space Pirate Panto

William Tell, The Panto

Novels

Heartsong

Get Santa: The Novel

Undefinable

Short Stories and Plot Outlines that would make GREAT FILMS, Mr Steven Spielberg, Sir

Quick Comedy Sketches for Young Comedians {as performed at "The Paragon Spectacular, White Rock Theatre, Hastings}

The Quiz That Keeps on Giving. A Charity Fund Raiser

JPR Williams X-Rayed my Head

Printed in Great Britain
by Amazon

43329800R00036